For Your Soul

He took my place!

Steven W. Edwards

IN MEMORY OF
~ELSIE MARIE PARISH~

May you rest in peace, to a woman who was my everything growing up.
Though you are gone, you are not forgotten. This is for you.

A Great Life
This is an example of what a great life was
Because there was not a nicer person than you.
In life that will take you a long way
We hate you had to pass away
My heart will never be okay.
I miss seeing and talking to you each day
Now you great life with Jesus begins
You're with the LORD and your pain can finally end
A new body and Life
On earth you were a great wife.
You were a great mother and friend
We hate your life had to end
That means your new life with Jesus will begin
The love you showed us will always shine through
No matter what we decide to do
For so many things I want to say I love you
Though you're gone my love for you will shine on
You will not be forgotten
We love you

Elsie Marie Parish a great Wife, Mother, Mother-in-law, Grandmother
She was just so many things for so many people. She served our country
proud. She passed her love of our country to her sons. Every day that
passes we will miss you. PS: While you're in heaven say hello to my son.
You had to go through a lot, but you finally got to meet Jesus!

Steven W. Edwards

IN MEMORY OF
~MELBA ANN BROOKS~
LOVE YOU ANYWAY

I know it must be great to be at home.
I hope you are looking at Jesus on the throne.
We still hurt because you're gone,
But someday we will be there too.
So that makes me very glad for you.
I wish you could tell me what heaven looks like.
From night to day and day to night
Oh my God, It must be a sight.
I know how close you were to God.
I know you held him close to your heart.
There were good times when I worked for you.
There were also hard times too.
We didn't see eye to eye some days,
We loved you anyway

To a great wife, mother, mother in law, Grandmother, and friend
She was so many things to so many people.

Table of Contents

For Your Soul

Introduction

I'm Steven Edwards. This is my book, and I hope it touches your soul like it touched mine by just writing it. When you open your heart healing begins. This book cannot get you to heaven. It will show you a pathway on which to travel. Only God can save you when you turn your heart to Him.

If you read this book you will see what God did for me. He can do the same for you. I was a man lost in this world mercy saved me. I thank God every day for this. I wonder, how do you thank someone that died for you? All I can do is live for him. This book is a testimony of that.

Some of the poems are about my life. Some are about others whom I've met and helped along the way.

I thank God for this blessing and gift to write a book. If you think this book is great, Thank God! I want to thank my pastor, Bro. Truman Carter who taught me so much. I want to thank my friend, and sister in Christ, Nicole who is also my publisher. I want to thank my friends at United Furniture for sticking by me all these years. I want to thank my mom, whom I love.

So start reading. I know you'll love it just as much as I did when I wrote it.

Dies in Regrets

There will be a lot of people in this world,
who will die in regret,
Not telling someone how they felt,
They'll go on until they are already dead,
Then it`s too late for anything to be said!
If you didn`t like someone how could you be
At the funeral talking about how close you used to be
saying you will be the one who misses them the most
You're so in spirit, in the holy ghost
and everyone there knows it`s a lie,
even if you do stand up and cry,
so why get up there and even try,
If what you say comes from the heart,
and you say what you mean, I'll accept that part
Just don't do it to be seen
You should have said it while they were living
When you don't it all sounds like lies,
even behind those crying eyes,
so say what you need to before they're dead,
then when they die you want feel as bad,
because everything will have already been said

3

Hide From Yourself

Most of the time if you don't want to be seen,
you can always hide,
but you must feel like an animal in a cage,
always locked and hidden away
how can you hide from yourself, behind your own eyes
that is where the real problems lies,
maybe you can hide from the world,
but you want be able to hide for long,
after a while of being all alone,
you will be trying to find someone to share your home,
because like I said, no one wants to be alone!
In life you can run and hide from place to place,
but how can you hide from your own face?

What is a church

What is a Church,
Is it just the place where we go
is it a place where people go to grow
The Church is the people that live inside
If they leave, the building will eventually die
Without any purpose for that building at all
The building will surely fall
How do you know if a Church is real
I say, just look in the people`s hearts
because that is really where the Church starts
You must open up your heart so you can really see
because if the Church is really inside you like you say
you'll carry the Church with pride and with you every day!
The Lord`s Church is the best one of all,
His Church is so strong and will never fall
Fire can`t burn it out
Water cannot drown it out
No matter what anyone tries to do
God's church will always be true
This Church comes from within,
and it starts when Jesus Christ becomes your friend!

A Bad Loser

In life you can`t always win, but you can always try again,
It does not matter what you are doing,
someone must always lose,
Someone must always win,
but when you lose don`t be a bad friend,
don't get all mad when you lose,
That wouldn`t be the right path to choose,
When you lose, lose with pride,
set all of your mad feelings aside,
if your madness supersedes
Go away hurry up and leave,
no one likes people that act that way,
why be a bad loser anyway?
I know sometimes when you lose, your ego gets a little
bruised,
but when you lose
Don`t act a fool,
just take your loss and keep your cool,
you can always try again,
and that will be your biggest win,
knowing when you lose you can always try again!

Say Hi

I must say to our Christians,
I`m very disappointed in you,
I cannot tell you from the world,
please give me some kind of clue,
I've see you pass someone by,
Not waving a hand or saying hi,
so what if that person has less than you,
is that what God told you to do?
When you pass someone,
you should look into their eyes
Don't let them think you're stuck up,
don't leave them wondering why,
Ignoring someone may make them cry
and just because you didn't say hi
Since you're too good to wave your hand
do you really think that is following God`s plan?
So next time you pass a bum on the street,
Wave your hand, say hi, give them something to eat!

The First of His Kind

There was only one Man that was one of a kind,
He had no sin and came down from on high
His job here was to mend
Not a shirt or tie or a pair of pants
This Man he mended souls with his blessed hands
To prove himself he had to die
to show the world he was not a lie,
He did this for you and me,
If you believe your soul will be free,
To me that is love in a whole new degree!
This Man I`m talking about is named Jesus,
and as long as we believe He will be with us,
He didn't put up a fight, cry, or fuss
but our love for Him must always be strong,
Jesus loves us even when we're wrong,
He's trying to show us the way home
On our journey there is a cross to bear,
but if we keep moving someday we will get there!

I'm Sorry

Sometimes I`m sorry just doesn't take the cake,
you never think about the hearts you break,
Sometimes I`m sorry just doesn`t work,
because of what you did, and the people you hurt,
what did you think I'm sorry will do
cause all the pain you caused to undo
Saying you are sorry is a good start,
but what can I do with this broken heart,
so saying you're sorry is good to hear,
but in my heart the pain is still near,
I was left all alone,
With no real place to call my home,
somehow I made it on my own!
I`m sorry is so easy to say,
I guess that`s why they're used so much in play,
and never meant from day to day,
I`m sorry does not always fix it,
because if you tell the Police I`m sorry,
you will still get a ticket!

United At United

Who would ever think we would meet this way,
We were just going to work
and living our life from day to day,
but when I met you I felt something new,
I knew someday I would love you,
nobody since has even came close
to making me feel the same,
and I only have our love to blame,
but who could have known,
how far one date would have gone,
we have been together ever since that day,
I guess our love was really meant to stay,
still it`s funny us meeting up this way,
I thank God for it each and every day,
that`s why I`m asking you in the same place we met,
"Marry me!" you're one thing in my life I won`t regret!

The Stars

Some people say the stars are the floors of Heaven,
They say because the gold floors are so bright,
we can only see the stars at night,
the sun shines so bright during the day,
No one would see them anyway!
But at night…you see all the stars shine
All over the world at the same time,
I don't know about you but this blows my mind,
Have you ever tried to count the stars in the sky
Looking at the sky I see why
None of the stars are the same,
God is the one you can blame,
Blaming God in this case is okay
Because He made them that way,
Sometimes I wish I could fly to mars
Maybe then I can touch the stars

A Love So True

I have a love so true,
my heart sometimes doesn't know what to do!
Every time you are around, my heart skips a beat,
Baby you are my own special treat!
A love so true,
I could not believe this love finally came,
now my life will never be the same!
A Love so true,
I would never want to see it end,
because each day I fall in love with you all over again,
A Love so true,
I knew you were handpicked by God for me,
this is why our love will always be,
I finally found a true love for me!

A Good Plan

Everyone in life must have some kind of plan
so you won't have to struggle
you try to make it the best you can
but first you must start with a good life plan,
and always be nice to your fellow man!
What is it you want the most in life,
maybe it has already past you by,
but if what you want is not yet here,
don't give up it is very near!
If you really want a good plan for your life,
Wait on God see what he's got
let's face it.
On your own you really haven't got a lot
That is okay,
God likes it better that way,
Then you can tell others where you have been,
Then maybe you can lead others away from sin,
Then your journey to Heaven will begin!

When I get Home

When you come home from a hard day's work,
being alone starts to really hurt
There is nothing to come home to each day,
Every day of the week all feels the same way
You're never in any hurry to go home,
because you know you will be all alone,
sooner or later the standoff has got to end
Into the lonely house you must go in
in you go to this empty house,
with everything in it as quiet as a mouse,
God said anything worth having, is worth working for,
One day I'll love opening my home door
One day I want be lonely anymore,
I will be happy again like before,
then there will be no pain in my heart anymore

Save a Church

Can you save a church,
or the people inside?
Is it a place for the sinner to go and hide?
Can you save a sinner,
that does not want to be saved?
Some people are saved only in their mind,
going through life thinking everything is just fine!
Can you save a church that goes to church to be seen
and not to get their souls redeemed?
Save a church!
You might save a soul!
Only if the Lord above is in control!

Never too Late

Most people think it is too late,
To learn something old or new
I don't care how old or smart
Something can always be taught to you
first you must be willing to learn,
you must be willing to take a little advice,
and then somehow your life might turn out alright!
It's never too late whatever you decide to do,
as long as you pray and have the Lord guiding you,
there is nothing in life that can block your way,
because the Lord will be there each and every day!
Wisdom comes in places you never think to look,
Wisdom does not always come from a book,
Wisdom can come from a small little child,
as smart as you are these ideas may seem kind of wild,
but all you have to do is listen and you will see
It is never too late to learn and smarter you will be

Being Immortal

Most people will say when you die it`s all over and done,
that is the end of the world your life and fun,
Not if you lived while you were here.
Helped out people and always give.
You will see that will get you a long way!
Look at so many people from back in the day
Movie Stars, War heroes, Authors, Bible Men and Women
The greatest of all was Jesus Christ from heaven.
They all left legacies though they are dead and gone,
their legacy still shines on
Every time you see a cross,
You think of Jesus and the blood He lost,
You think how he died for you and me
So our souls could be set free
their stories continue to be told
Even once they're dead and gone
their stories give them immortality
They still reach out to you and me
There is something to be said,
When your soul reaches a person from the dead

Real or Play

When you say things are you for real
or are you playing with how you feel
are you talking bad about a man
hoping you'll never see him again.
Can you live what you say, or are all your words just talk
and play
The way you live is all people see,
so I live my life so man can believe
Like I'm ready to go home,
to a far better place,
where I can finally see God's face,
what a wonderful day that day will be
then it will be just God and me,
then He can tell me if I have done wrong,
and If my life was good enough to call heaven home
when your time is up money won't save you,
so in the end it's all about people and love,
and that is the only way you will ever see above
this crime and hate,
so bow your head and wait on God because He will never
be late!

Faith or Fake

Do you have real faith in God your maker,
or are you like most of the world a big faker?
If you don't have faith you don't have a lot
Regardless of how much money you've got
because if your heart is fake your fate will be the same
as someone who never even heard God's name!
When a man or woman has no faith at all
Everything around them will soon start to fall
It will happen with no warning in sight
In life sometimes things can seem so right,
It could be the very thing that is all wrong
It's keeping your heart from having faith,
and not allowing your soul to go home,
so faith or fake the choice is in your hands
but if I were you, I would have faith in God's plan

Confusing Love

Why does love have to be so confusing,
It always seems to have you choosing
between the love we had,
and the love we got,
and these days that love does not seem to be a lot!
Sure I know you really care,
but is your love for me still there,
because this is a confusing love,
and these are some confusing times,
always having to wonder is your love really mine,
and if it is will our love be just fine,
and will our love be the love,
that will stand the test of time?
This is a confusing love,
but still I must see if your love is true,
because my heart really does love you!

Love by The Minute

Sometimes love can feel one way one minute,
and another way the next,
Who can really say which way is best
everyone must fall in love on their own
No one person can say what's right or wrong
Nobody ever feels the same pain,
When you are in love, You do strange things
No one can say who is wrong or who is right,
Neither of us cares when we get into a fight,
I think are we in love or is it just lust
I guess I am asking what's all the fighting worth
In life sometimes one night is all you need
to tell if this love is the love you need
Sometimes love doesn't feel the same
When that happens who can you really blame

Happy 32nd Anniversary

Happy 32 Anniversary Mom and Pop,
We wanted you to know this family loves you a lot
This love this family shares is what it's really about
We just want to thank you for the time you gave,
to the wonderful children that you raised
and for making sure we got plenty to eat,
at night having us a warm place to sleep
all the things you did without money just faith
in our mines these things will never be erased,
that is why in our hearts we cover you with grace
Mom and Pop your love will always hold a special place!
Happy 32 Anniversary and we hope you have 32 more,
and we hope each year will be better than before
you two just think 32 years ago,
did either of you really know,
how far this love could really go?
Happy 32 Anniversary from your family with love!

Home

Most people will say home is just a place to stay,
but if you have love at home,
I`m sure you would not feel this way,
"Home is where the heart is" I heard a wise man say,
So everywhere I go I should make it my home place
There are some people who are on their own
In this world all alone,
with no real place to call their home,
so I guess your home is where you make it in the end,
for a reminder your home is also where it all begins

Plant the Seed

In life all you can do is plant your seeds,
Sit back watch it grow and pull up the weeds
because not all seeds will ever grow the same,
that is why not all seeds have the same name,
and this also goes for your children too,
because whatever you do they will be watching you
They'll watch you do wrong with no shame
Then who can you blame when your kids act the same?
When you argue, fight, fuss, and cuss,
Your kids see and hear. It's so unjust
The sad part is they're the ones who suffer the most
The very ones we should hold dear
when you plant a seed in a garden,
It needs water and sunlight to grow
but to plant a seed in a child's life you must be willing to show
a lot of love, and caring and some of your time,
and that is the only way the seed you plant will turn out fine!

In This Time

In this time is where you need someone to help you,
and a good friend just to talk to
In this time is where you need a real friend
while you let your healing begin,
I will be that friend to the end,
through all the pain and tears,
I don`t care if it takes months or years!
In this time your pain may be hard for you to bear,
but know you have people who loves you and will always
be there!
In this time I guess you have had a lot of time to think,
about how your life can change in just one blink?
In this time is where you must be strong,
so you can get through this and carry on!
In this time is where you need to believe in God,
and what He can really do,
and I promise God will have a blessing waiting on you,
and God will make you better than new!

Life's has a meaning

What does your life mean,
Each day it can seem like the same old thing!
Don't feel that way you have a destiny
You just don't know yet what you'll be
Stop wasting time one day you will see
God has a purpose for each life on earth,
God made these plans long before your birth,
at first no one knows what there life is meant for,
Give your life to God
You won't wonder anymore
God will open up your eyes,
and take away the lies,
You true life will appear before your eyes
Take this message and use it right
and then you can really see,
what your life was meant to be!

Listen to your kids

Parents do you know who your kid is
Or is your name the only thing you give
If that is really all you claim
you'll be a bad parent
with no one else to blame
Walking around the house everyday
and we never have anything good to say,
and we wonder why our kids act the same way!
Parents just listen to your kids,
and see what that day they did,
Parents you only get one change to be a father or mother
Find different ways to say you love them
and children when your parents tell you what to do,
they are only telling you because they love you,
Try everyone to listen to each other

God's Enforcers

In life we must be God's enforcers if we care at all,
If not our lives and everything around us will fall,
and sometimes it will happen with no warning at all
and only God knows why you were chose
He knows why your hand he holds
Since you are chosen you must do your best
Keep your hand in His you will be blessed
As God's Enforcer in heaven you will rest.
One day in heaven you'll be welcomed in
from your long journey to heaven
You will have set lost souls free
showing them their sins are forgiven
The people you helped were just like you
Because of your faith everyone got through!

Hot List to Hell

Is your name on the hot list to Hell
If it is you better get it off soon,
before it`s too late and you meet your doom!
The hot list to Hell is miles and miles long,
but you can take a different path of your own,
and this path will lead you to Heaven,
where your name really belongs,
you don`t have to have your name on the hot list to Hell,
If you don`t see fit to,
because at any time God can save you!
I know when you made your life`s plans,
this is not at all what you meant,
but if you want to make it better,
just get on your knees and repent,
for all of your sins,
and that`s when your road to Heaven will really begin!

Free Your Soul

Do you ever think there`s more to life than you see,
and what about your soul is it free?
Do you think about what will happen to your soul,
if when you die God was not in control?
Do you think about your soul a lot,
if you don`t you are heading for where it is hot,
to that long ride to the fire,
and that is not what any soul would ever desire,
but if you have a free soul,
that means you let God back in control,
and it is a good thing that you did,
because now your soul is free and hide,
because if you keep your soul behind God,
and away from enemy lines,
and then when you die your soul will be just fine!

The Victory

If you stick with God all your life
when you die the victory is yours
because you can finally walk through Heaven`s doors,
and walk on golden floors
This victory is not an easy one
Getting there will not always be fun
 If you want to get to Heaven,
there is much work to be done
this victory in life cannot be bought or sold,
many will not have it no matter how old
They were not living their life right,
and never had a good plan in sight,
No worries your victory is always there,
Just take the time to travel with care
This victory has a long road ahead
Go with God and always be lead

Pick and Choosing

In life you have to pick and choose,
your battles in life,
but your battles must be worth the fight,
because if you fight a lot of worthless battles in life,
one of your worthless battles might get the best of you,
and then your life on earth will be through!
What is it on earth you hate the most and just cannot stand,
or do you try to be nice to every fellow man,
because if you fight everyone you don`t like,
sooner or later you will need a grave site,
because you lost the fight and your life at the same time,
and now your family is about to lose their mind,
and all because you did not pick and choose,
and that means most of the time you will lose!

The First of His Time

There was only 1 man that was 1 of a kind,
that did no sin,
and made a lot of friends,
because in His job He mends,
but it is not a pair of pants,
or a shirt or a tie,
this man, He mends souls,
and to prove it he had to die,
to show the world he was not a lie,
and of course for you and me,
where if you believe your soul will be free,
and to me that is love to a whole new degree!
This Man I`m talking about is named Jesus,
and as long as we believe he will be with us,
without any problems or fuss,
but our love for him must always be strong,
and Jesus will love us even when you do wrong,
because all he is trying to do is show us the way home,
but first everyone has a journey we must bear,
but if we keep moving someday we will all get there!

How is it going to Look

How is it going to look
when the Lord comes back
and we have not read His book?
Never obeyed
what the Lord had to say.
How is it going to look
when you want feed someone in need?
How are you going to sound
when the Lord hits the ground?
How are you going to look
when your name isn't written in the Lord's book?
There is no need to run or hide,
because the Lord is right by your side.
How is it going to look
with the devil as your cook?

Lover's and Friends

Can you really be lover`s and friends
at the same time, if you can
you got a strong mind,
because once you become a lover,
there is no keeping this love uncover,
and there is no going back to being just a friend,
because you will want to be a lover all over again,
then when the other person don`t feel the same,
who can your heart really blame,
then your heart can never win,
when all she wants to be is a friend!
Lover`s and Friends, can you be both at the same time,
or will you eventually lose your mind?

Lead and Follow

We need to lead the people away from sin,
Get them to believe in God once again!
It was a time people cared,
about Jesus dying on that cross so long ago,
now most people just say so!
Will you lead or will you follow the world,
when it`s left without any kind of clue,
and everyone is asking is what I believed in even been true!
Will you lead the people away from God`s plan,
or will they be able to follow you to Heaven
to God`s promised land?
Lead or follow that is a big choice you must make,
but you are dealing with God,
so do not try to make your decision to late!

Heaven's Floor

When you open up Heaven's doors,
gold is all on the floors,
gold all at your feet,
and all the food you could want to eat!
Tables of food as far as my eyes could look
these things you only read in a book!
I walked on Heaven's floors
in what seem for about 100 miles,
and all I could see was nothing
but friendly smiles. I saw a bright
light above, and I knew it was
the Lord that I had heard of.
God said come my child
and do not be afraid,
I'm here to come to your aid!
God said take this body, and do it proud,
and make sure you say it loud!
Then God said son if you want to make it
back to Heaven's floors, stick with me
and the key to Heaven will be yours!

Forgive and Forget

We can forgive, but can we forget sometimes we pretend
we forgive and everything is just fine
but you really do not like them all the time!
Sometimes it is really easy to forgive
but why is it so hard to forget?
But you must forgive that person,
so you do not live your life in regret!
Because if a person does you wrong
they are just preventing them self from going home!
So just forgive that person for what they have done,
so you can live your life and have some fun!
Sometimes loved ones do some crazy things
without any warning at all,
but do not make that a reason not to call!
In life you have to forgive people for what they say,
because it really don`t matter anyway,
but if you forgive someone today,
you will see God will always show you a better way!
But why can we forgive, but seem to never forget?

When I get Myself to Heaven

When I get home what a wonderful day this will be,
it will be just The Lord and me,
I will be happy because my soul will be free!
When I get home, all my problems will be gone,
Because my soul is already saved I can meet my maker
I won`t be in for that terrible heartbreaker!
When I get home from this life in Hell,
all I can only hope is I served my Father well,
and He loves me enough not to send my soul to that fiery
hell!
When I get home from for all this heartache and pain,
and I meet God face to face then I will know
my journey was not in vain,
and now I can finally get awarded for my pain!
When I get home there will be no more tears in my eyes,
and no more pain on my face,
because for once I will be in a very happy place,
back with my maker in God`s loving grace!

Sinner and a Saint

Do you know the difference between a sinner and a saint?
A sinner and a saint,
some people will say they are one in the same,
but I think that just depends on your name,
and if you can handle blame and shame
for calling yourself a saint knowing you still sin,
but you don`t have to worry,
because Jesus will always be your friend,
and this is a friendship that will last beyond the grave,
to the Heavens and beyond the sky,
and why Jesus loves us so I guess we will never know
why?
I have always wondered can you fake being a sinner,
and make people think you are a saint,
when everyone knows you really aint?
I guess all I'm saying is be careful
when you call yourself a saint,
and in your heart you know you really aren't
because God can always work through the sin
but in your heart you cannot pretend!

Time and Money

Do you ever stop and just listen to how most people talk?
If you do you will find most people thinks about the same way,
if you want my time you must pay,
and how much money depends on how big the job is,
because they say nothing in life is free,
but I must disagree,
because God's love comes free of charge,
but a lot of your bad habits you must discard,
this is a hard task you must do,
but keep your faith up, and always remember God's loves you,
no matter what in life you might you try to do?
sometimes we do so much bad we just say,
why bother with God anyway,
but I tell you God will love you through it all,
even when you are down and out and ready to fall,
all you have to is just call His name,
and God will be there like you just made a 911 call,
and God will lift you out of harm's way,
and show you His love will never go away,
no matter what someone else might say!

Merry Christmas

Merry Christmas to each and every one,
and I hope this year you have a lot of love and fun,
and I hope this year all your dreams come true,
no matter what this Christmas you decide to do,
Christmas time should be filled with plenty of love,
because that is what God showed us
when He sent His son from above!
Maybe this year we will try to be nice and not so mean,
and I bet you will enjoy Christmas a lot more,
and this will be a Christmas like you have never had
before!
This year have yourself a big smile,
and give someone a big hug on this Christmas day,
and you will see that smile and hug will go a long way,
and it would not hurt if you took time out to pray,
and thank God for sending His love our way!
Merry Christmas and have a happy new year!

Betting on Time

Betting on time,
is what a lot of people still do,
but is this the right thing for you?
Betting on time,
not knowing how much time is left
never knowing you could be taking
your last breathe! betting on time
playing Russian roulette with your soul
maybe it`s time for you to let God
take control? Betting on time,
not knowing when death could strike
it might be a good time to get your soul right!
Betting on time, a bet you will surely lose,
if the Lord above is not what you decide to choose!
Betting on time,
and waiting for your untimely death
but if you turn your life to God,
your soul will not be doomed
to hell like the rest!

New Dream

Most people today,
they live life the same old way.
Most people stop trying to chase their dreams,
and just takes life as it seems.
No man can help you when you pray,
so why do you need an approval of a man today?
New dreams,
are never what they seem!
New dreams,
always look to see,
what the world has to offer me.
If you try a new way of sight,
maybe one day the Lord will get your soul right.
New dreams can be very bad,
but think of all the good dreams you had.
When you have a new dream of death,
wake up and catch your breath.

My Love

I wrote this poem to let you know,
my love for you will never go.
The love I have for you in my heart
can never be torn apart.
When I awake up from the morning light,
your face is what I want in my sight.
No other person can tear me away,
my love will always stay.
I cannot wait till I get home from a hard day,
because I know you are waiting to make everything okay.
If you left me I would not know how to act,
every day I would try to get our love back.
When you look at the world and there is nothing good to
see,
remember my love will always be.
Through all the pain and through all the tears,
I hope our love will last many, many years.

We Won

We won, the war that is what people say,
but what was we fighting for anyway?
A lot of soldiers lost their lives,
and cannot go home to their husbands and wives.
We won, but what about the children that are home sad,
because they can never see their mom or dad.
We won, but what did we really win?
A loss of a husband or wife or friend.
We won, but what about the lonely wife crying in bed,
because her husband is dead?
We won, but we really lost,
because lives of soldiers is a big cost.
We won ,so guess I need to shout,
and let the good news out, WE WON!

A Say

Do I have a say,
in what you are about to do,
I need to know is your love really true?
Do I have a say, in where our love will go from here,
or will our love just fade away, and disappear?
Do I have a say,
in what decision your heart is about to make,
or for me did I wait too late?
Do I have a say,
can my love change your heart,
or will our love just break away and fall apart?
Do I have a say,
or is there nothing left to be said,
or will our love die away,
leaving my heart feeling numb and dead?

Goodbye 2006

Good bye 2006 you really put this county in a bad fix,
2007 has to be the year we turn it around,
but people`s heads must be on solid ground!
Good bye 2006 I can`t say you will be missed
because a lot of lives will be forever lost,
believe me 2006 came with a great cost,
but I`m still here standing proud,
like a lost person mixed in with the crowd,
I`m here but I don`t know which way I`m supposed to go,
it`s like in 2006 everyone just lost their flow,
good bye 2006 we will never see your date
on our calendar again,
so maybe in 2007 we can let some of the healing begin!
Happy New Year!

Faith Test

What is a faith test, you ask me?
It`s a test from God to see how faithful you will be!
Will you lie, or even steal,
or will you follow God up that lonely old hill,
to that old rugged cross,
where your life might be lost!
Will you pass that faithful test,
or will your be lost in Hell with all the rest?
This is a hard test you must try to do,
but if you pass this test,
the two keys to Heaven will be given to you!

A Part of Life

Something's in life are just a part of life,
and there is nothing you can do,
like changing a dirty diaper,
because you know the baby cannot change themselves,
just like going to work and paying the bills,
that is just one of life's little deals,
and whether you want it or not,
these things will keep coming a lot,
sometimes life can be funny or sad,
but there is no need of getting mad,
because these things are just a part of life,
that must be done,
because certain things is just a part of life,
it's just something that you must do,
and it happens to everyone in life not just you!

Life Without Christ

Life without Christ would be,
something unpleasant no one should have to see.
When you get old,
your life will become very cold.
No one cares if you live or die,
or even stops by to say hi.
Life without Christ for you will be very sad,
because for some reason you are always mad.
Christ can turn all of that around,
and help you get your feet on the ground!
You need to seek Christ very soon,
before you lose sight of the moon!
Life without Christ is not very bright,
there is nothing left to look forward to at night.
Life with Christ is very great,
because you do not have to live in the devil's lake.
Walk with Christ and you will see,
there is nothing you cannot be!
Christ is waiting for that day,
to take you home and wash all your sorrows away!

My Family and Friends

Family and Friends, are always supposed to be,
but that is not want we always see.
Family is someone you can cherish through it all,
and will never let you fall.
Family should help you when you frown,
and should never let you stay down.
True friends are hard to come by,
a true Friend will never try to make you cry.
If you get thrown in jail,
a true friend will go your bail.
Family and Friends, are always supposed to stay,
and suppose to show you how to live the right way.
When Family and Friends, decide to stray away,
The Lord is the only one who will be there from day to day.
When you have a secret to deep,
remember there`s nothing the Lord can`t keep.

Nothing But You

Nothing but you,
all through my lonely day,
my heart is always longing for you,
baby tell me you love me too!
Even when I try to turn my feelings away,
you are all I can think about from day to day!
When I look around, I see nothing but your face,
and every time I see you, my heart starts to race!
Nothing but you, is all my heart seems to know,
baby when I get you I promise I won`t ever let you go!
Nothing but you, is all my heart is looking for,
Baby I love you,
and I don`t want to hide my feelings for you anymore!

Soul on Fire

Soul on fire,
is a desire for my soul.
Fire burning in my soul,
now let the Lord Take control.
Fire in my soul burning deep,
this is a feeling I want to keep.
The Lord knocks on your soul every day,
and most of the time we still turn him away.
If the Lord came back today,
a lot of people would try to run away.
If your soul is not on track,
don`t worry the Lord is waiting to put it back.

A Smile

If you give someone a smile,
that is something that will last a lot of miles.
If walk around with a frown,
it will always keep you down!
Even if you wear a frown,
your bills is still coming around.
You might as well wear a smile today,
because all you have to do is knell down and pray!
A smile can go a long way to a person who is all alone,
that smile may make them feel at home.
So smile while you are in this place,
and hope God is smiling when He sees your face.
When you have no smile to be found,
remember the Lord can bring it back around.

A Mother's Love

A Mother's love will always be,
and when you feel sad and all alone,
she is always the first one you want to see,
because she will dry my eyes and take good care of me,
and every time my life starts to fall,
I know I can just give my Mother a call,
because a Mother`s love will last through it all,
and when my Mother goes to her final resting place,
God will be so proud to meet my Mother face to face,
but for now she still has to run life`s race,
with the devil on the chase,
and after that all her suffering will be gone,
and she will be with God in her new home!

Take One Last Look

Take one last look!
At what the lord has took.
Do not feel sad,
because the person that passed is glad.
They are gone away.
Left us feeling like we need to pray.
They loved life why they were here,
but now their life will disappear.
Look at this body and look at this face,
and after this they will be with grace.
When you feel all alone do not worry.
Someday the lord will take you home.
Take one last look at this body today,
and remember tomorrow death might come your way.
The only way to save your soul,
is to let God take control.

Sunday Sinner

Sunday comes looking nice,
and we tell the Lord we are going to do right.
Sunday comes we always pray,
Lord give us a better day.
Monday comes we do like we like,
and we forgot we told the Lord we was going to do right.
Tuesday comes same old thing.
Running around acting insane.
Wednesday comes we are always down,
because we have no money to go to town.
Thursday comes it seems alright,
but when is the Lord going to get His night?
Friday is here time to unwind,
but when is the Lord going to get his time?
Saturday is here and it`s time to act a fool,
and we get in them streets and try to act so cool.
Sunday is here time to pray,
but what about every other day?

Brighter Days

There are brighter days ahead,
because you are not dead.
Even at night,
when things will not get right.
Even if you are broke,
someone will still buy you a coke.
Even when you are down,
don`t hit the ground.
Even after death,
don`t lose your breath.
Even when you fall,
the Lord is still waiting for your call,
because there are brighter days

Approval of God

Approval of God is what we need,
because He is the one who had to bleed.
If you always remember to pray,
the Lord will never go away.
Approval by man,
that is not the right plan.
Approval of God is very rare,
and some people don`t even care.
Approval by man is what we seek,
but the Lord will show us that leak.
God is the only one with the book,
no one else will be able to take a look.
Approval by God is what will stay!
Approval by man want last a day.
When God puts a stamp on your heart,
no man or his money can tear it apart.
When it is time to see God`s face,
remember no man can take His place.

Starting Over

I know starting over is hard for you,
but in life it`s something we all must do.
Everything is different now you are gone,
now I`m wonder how I can go on?
Lord why did you take my loved one away from me?
I wish their death didn`t have to be.
Starting new things is very hard,
it`s like opening a new deck of cards.
Never knowing what is going to turn up,
till you turn over and see you have messed up!
Then you need to start over again,
but don`t not give in,
and then someday you will truly win.
When you have trouble starting over,
after a loved one has passed away,
remember God is waiting to help you start over,
and to find something to substitute your pain away.

Money Can Pay

money can pay for a life
and can pay for a death
money can buy you a new eye
but cannot buy the sky
you need money every day but you have
to use it the right way
money can get you thrown in jail
do not worry there is always bail
money can bring
a lot of nice things
money can pay your way in life
but what is the lords price
when your day comes and you go away
what will you be able to pay

Down on Your Luck

When you get down on your luck,
you never have enough bucks.
Living life the same old way,
I might try to pray.
Hoping one day the Lord,
will show me a better way.
Throw the dice and bet on seven,
but how is this getting us to Heaven?
Luck will drive you insane,
because it is all in vain.
If you drop the act,
the Lord will take your soul back.
Luck is something we want to say,
but all we have to do is pray.
There is no luck to be found,
when the Lord is around.

1 Year Anniversary

I wrote this to let you know,
my love will never go.
No one else can come close to taking your place.
My heart gets lost just looking at your beautiful face!
When we got married I knew our love was true,
because I did not want anybody but you.
I am glad we share the love we share.
It shows how much my heart truly cares.
Never forget the first time we kissed!
I knew God had granted me a wish.
I love you dear this is true,
without you my heart would not know what to do.
When I wake up at night,
you are the first thing I want in my sight.
I love it when we lock the doors
and go inside and make some noise.
1 year has passed since that faithful day
I am glad we decided to stay.
Happy Anniversary.

Wind Blows

wind blows through it all
spring summer winter and fall
wind blows sometimes cold and sometimes hot
be sure to know it blows a lot
wind blows at night and is still blowing
when it gets light
wind does not care what it blows away
so you better stay out of its way
wind can get strong
and blow down your home
if you see a storm coming your way
duck down or it will knock you out of the way

Angel Ahead

Angels are with you at night,
to help you see the light.
Angels are with you during the day,
trying to show you a better way.
Even when you get drunk at a bar,
Angels will help you drive your car.
You can feel Angels in your heart,
and no man can tear that apart.
When you are feeling down,
Angels will always be around.
Angels are here for you,
to show you what God wants you to do.
Angels are ahead when you walk,
all they want, is for you and God to have a talk.
Angels are sent by The Man,
so you better follow your Angel,
and get with the Lord`s plan!

Money Times

Money time is here,
no times for games or fear,
everyone is looking to see,
what you are trying to be,
there is no time for sorrow
because there is no tomorrow,
money time is waiting
for your taking,
the night is the night
so you better shine bright
when you feel like you are going to cry,
look up at the sky
grab the LORDS hand
and he will help you stand,
and He will help you put that money in your hands,
but only if you follow the Lord`s plans!

Labels

People label things by how they look,
but labels belong on a book.
You label a person because they do not fit in.
Never knowing where that person's life has been.
You get a little money,
and now you want to act funny.
Who are you to tell,
someone they are going to feel?
Label people by what they wear,
but clothes will always tear.
You label a person by what you see,
but who are you supposed to be?
You can get a bad label by a lie,
but no man can label you when you die.
Label a person by who they know,
but the Lord is still running the show.
You label a person because they are poor,
but what does the Lord have in store?
If the Lord puts a label on you today,
that is one label that can't be washed away.

Death

Death is something no one wants to see,
but this is how life must be.
Everyone is crying so many tears.
For the person who passed whom which had some good
years.
You could die today you never know.
The Lord could call you, would you be ready to go?
Death is good if you and the LORD are tight!
If not, it is going to be a bad sight.
If you keep the LORD in sight.
Your life will always turn out alright.
Death does not have a certain day.
So it's best to remember to always pray.
When death comes lingering your way.
It is too late to try to pray.
While you're running around acting so brave,
death is waiting to put you in a grave.
Death comes when you are doing great.
So do not get caught in the devil's lake.

If You Knew

If you only knew that this was your last day,
would you still be too proud to pray?
Would you begin undoing the bad?
That was done making people sad.
If you knew you was going to die,
would you ask the Lord why?
If you knew this was your last day,
would that make you get down on knees and pray?
If you knew you and this world had to part,
would you try to change your heart?
If the Lord called your name,
would you run away in shame?
If you knew this was your last night,
would you try to get your soul right?
If you knew the Lord wanted you today,
would you be ready to fly away?

Look In The Mirror

I look in the mirror, what do you see?
It's another person that looks just like me.
I look in the mirror, and I shake my head,
because in life I can never get ahead.
I look in the mirror, and say what a sight.
Is anything good going to happen to me tonight?
What you are looking at is hard to say,
but maybe tomorrow will be a better day.
If you look in the mirror in another place,
you will still see the same face.
When the mirror is too hard to bare,
remember the Lord is still there.
You can run from people, and you can run from a place,
but you can never run from your own face!

Kid's Today

What about our kids today,
too many trying throw their life away.
Not going to school,
because they say it`s not cool.
With no school, or no job,
the only thing left is to try to rob.
Growing up too fast,
but that life will never last.
By growing up this quick,
they think they are very slick.
Growing up too soon,
and having babies that are doomed.
A child can never know what is right,
with no parents in sight.
A dad at twelve,
will always fell!
Kids today don`t get the right start,
and think they are so smart.
Kids today need to stop and pray,
and listen to what God has to say.

The Devil

The Devil is around,
even when you go to town.
The Devil is slick,
because he works quickly.
Even as early as nine,
The Devil is already trying to take control of their mine.
The Devil is up 24 hours a day,
trying to make someone go astray.
God is always in your sight,
and always waiting for you to get your life right.
The Devil knows He can never be the Man,
so He tries to turn you away from God`s plan.
The Devil will make everything sound good for a day,
but if you follow the Devil someday the Lord will make
you pay.

Parents Today

Parents today have babies and run away,
in hopes the baby can wait till another day.
Parents today want their kids to pray,
but is never there to show them the way.
Parents want their kids to do right,
but they are never in sight.
Parents today are made to go to court,
before they will pay any child support.
Parents today tell kids what is right,
but do wrong in there sight.
Parents today some us are not so bright,
because some of us don`t know where our kids are at night.
Parents today run around all night,
and don`t see their kids until the sun gets bright.
Parents today we need to stop and pray,
because we cannot let our kids grow up this way

Time To Come Up

It`s time for me to come up,
and make some of these real bucks!
Always keep down,
but this time I`m coming off this Hell bounded ground!
When people hear these words,
they will tell others what they have heard!
I`m tired of taking orders from a man,
so I decided to follow the Lord`s Plan!
I`m going to come up from broke,
and I guess that sounds like a joke?
When I leave I will leave them haters behind,
and I will go to D.C. and try to shine!
When I go to D.C.
I will show the world what I can be!
I have been in this small town too many nights,
Now it`s time to go to D.C. and get right!
When I come back from D.C. and make a lot of money,
a lot of people will be looking funny!
For the people that never gave I a second look,
that is ok because I have wrote a book!

Happy Birthday

Happy Birthday,
this is your day.
Life isn`t always as it seems,
but keep reaching, and you will reach your dreams.
This is the day the Lord set aside,
so hold your head up in pride.
You made it one more year,
so be glad you are still here.
When your problems seem out of sight,
turn to the Lord, and He will make everything alright.
This is a Very Special Day,
so have a Happy Birthday.

Defend Myself

Judge I might as well defend myself today,
because my lawyer don`t care anyway!
I`m out on bail,
and I`m not trying to go back to jail!
I have been trying to give them their money,
but all they want to do is act funny.
Nobody is never listening to want I have to say,
but I`m the one who has to pay.
They are trying to make the court believe a bold face lie,
and they wouldn`t tell the truth if they were about to die!
So Judge, can I approach the Bench,
I got someone I need to fire!
Why? Judge that is what you are asking me?
Because He has not done one thing to keep me free!
Judge Please, have mercy on this face,
and God will surely reward you,
when you get to His Heavenly Place.

Something is Coming

something is coming very soon
to take me away from this doom
something is coming very quick
and I hope it is a nice lick
something is coming I hope and pray
and I hope it is coming my way
something is coming that I can keep this is a feeling
that is coming from down deep
something is coming to show me the way
because the LORD will never let me go astray
THE LORD is coming to answer my prays
because his love never tears
sometimes we think we lose the LORD when
we hide
but the LORD is always by your side

Their Records

their records shows one thing today
but my records show the right way
I have never seen records change overnight
I wish someone would shed me some light
they tell you what the records say
but then turn around and make you pay
if they cannot keep their records tight
how can they say mine are not right
they say their records say I took out
to much money
so I try to pay them back and they act funny
keeping up with the money is the banks job
so how can they say I tried to rob

The Law

where is the law when you are in need
somewhere doing what they call a good deed
the law is always there when you
take a drink
and looking at you every time you blink
if the law stops you and you are not right
it is not going to be a good night
the law will try to fill you with fears
and will try to fill your eyes with tears
the law is the one
who is support to save the day
but all they want for you is to pay
if you are in the wrong place
and try to pray
the law will try to lock you away

Wise In the Mind

when you are wise in the mind
no one should have to tell you what is
on their mind
you will know from the start
because you are so smart
just going through the day
saying what you want to say
always do your best
then sit down and take a rest
wise in the mind
but the kids mind is ahead of their times
wise in the mind if you step off the devils
burning floor
wise in the mind if you knock on the LORDS
door

Young Age

I am at a young age
but I am still trying to get paid
writing poems everyday
hoping GOD will show me a better way
standing around in the night
hoping to see some light
when you have a hard day
maybe you need to pray
going to town looking clean
but do not forget who gave you that ring
at a young age you are running fast
always wants to have a blast
at a young age you are going hard
because you do not want to play
like an old deck of cards

Home Sweet Home

When you are home,
you should never feel alone.
When you get off track,
home is where you can come back.
Home is where you can share,
and show people how to care.
Home is a place you can share your fears,
and you also can shed a few tears.
If your home was never right,
that may be the reason you want come home at night.
If you put the Lord in your home tonight,
by tomorrow everything will be alright.

Who Can Explain

who can explain
why stars come out at night
things that cannot be seen by sight
why we wake up in the morning
the LORD is so close
I can almost see his face
but I will wait till GOD invites me to grace
I have been close to death several times
but THE LORD takes my hand and said
wake up it is not your time
who can explain why your loved one dies
and not you
leaving you feeing lost and blue
the only way you really get it explain
right
you will have to get on your knees tonight

The Color

If a person has a different color,
should they be put in back with the others?
Who are you to say what color is right?
When everybody is the same color without the light.
The Lord Didn`t put your color on you for it to last a day.
That is the color the Lord put on you to stay.
How can you say you love the Lord today,
and hate someone because their color don`t look your way?
The Lord makes every color in the book,
so stop judging color and give that a look!
The Lord is watching you every day,
so don`t be so quick to turn His children away.

How Do You Know

it is time to go
and hit my flow
people ask me
how do you know this is to be
because THE LORD is in control
and running my soul
with THE LORD in my heart
no man can tear me apart
I pray every day
LORD show me a better way
THE LORD is in sight
and shinning bright with that heavenly light
how do I know what I will be
I will follow THE LORD and then we will see

This Job

I`s time for me to leave this Job,
I have made enough money I don`t have to rob,
It was a new adventure every day,
after I started to pray.
Now I got my life right,
and now I can shine bright.
The Lord is with me every day,
to show me the right way.
When I leave don`t be sad,
just think of the good memories we all had.
Now it`s time for me to step down,
and leave this company ground.
Then I will be gone for a lot of days,
and then I will come back and see who stays.
When I come back with a lot of money,
a lot of people is going to look funny.

But Thank God

You are lying in bed,
but thank God you are not dead.
At this moment you can`t walk,
but thank God you can still talk.
You had a bad wreck, and you lived to tell,
but thank God His love didn`t fell.
The wreck may have got glass in your eye,
but thank God He didn`t let you die.
Your body is hurt and at this moment you cannot drive,
but thank God you are still alive.
When you are lying in bed today,
remember to thank God and always pray.
The Lord loves you He showed you so,
so thank God He didn`t let you go.

10 Signs of a Christian

They go to church to pray,
and they always have something nice to say.
They always find a way to overcome the bad,
and try to keep others from being sad.
They give to others before themselves,
and don`t put people`s business on display selves,
A true Christian want be trying to hurt people in anyway,
and will give someone a warm place to stay.
A true Christian can fellowship with all colors of life,
and want be trying to take some man`s wife.
A true Christian can love all different colors the same,
and will never call people out of their name.
A true Christian want be trying to break up homes,
and tries to help people not feel so alone.
A true Christian always tries to do what is right,
and their relationship with God is very tight.
A true Christian you can tell how God has changed their heart,
and always know no man can pick that apart.

Follow the World

Follow the world and you will see,
what God does not want you to be.
Follow a world with no hope,
God will still waiting to throw you a rope.
Everything the world does that is not right,
God can change it around overnight.
If you follow the world to make some quick money,
the Lord will not think that is funny.
Follow a world that looks nice,
but God will make you pay a big price.
You follow a world with no plan,
but God is still waiting to take you by the hand.
When you follow the world today,
the world will get you in trouble and run away.
Follow the Lord and you will be alright,
and you will see something good in sight.

Ready To Be Bumped

come home ready to bump
but all I see is this dump
come home ready to bump tonight
but my wife says she don't feel right
I am not trying to look in someone else face
because I want bump at no other place
when I wake up you are the first thing
in my sight-and then I know everything
will be alright and baby before you go
I would just like to know
can we bump tonight
and I will make you fill out of sight
I am home ready to bump
but before we do can you clean up this dump

Steven W. Edwards

What Kind of Plan

God what kind of plan,
is it for a man,
to have to eat food out of a garage can?
What kind of man,
walks around with no plan?
It sounds like a joke,
but this man is really broke.
How can this man cope,
walking around with no hope?
How can this man live this way,
maybe he needs to pray?
It makes me want to cry,
and ask the Lord why?
He doesn't want to rob,
but he has gave up on getting a job.
God how is this plan right,
this man does not have a place to sleep at night?
God please take this man,
and show him his life's plan.

My Father's Business

It`s time for me to stop my life and see,
is this what God would want me to be?
It`s time for me to step up to the plate,
before I die and it`s too late.
It`s time for me to take my place,
and tell others about God`s Grace!
It`s time to take God`s call,
and share God`s word with all.
I can`t allow myself to fell,
because I don`t want to see anyone end up in hell.
I`m going to lift up so many souls,
and show the people God is in control.
I`m going to be a better man,
and try to live by God`s plan.
I`m going to touch people`s soul,
and let them know in life they do have a goal.
Just follow God and He will help you see,
where in life He wants you to be!
In life you will see a lot of so call true love begin and end,
but The Lord is the only One that can,
save our soul and, forgive us of our sin!

Every Day At 5

every day at 5
it was a struggle to stay alive
every day at 5 I had to walk the same way
and I was told I could not pray
every day at 5 I would look in the sky
and would ask THE LORD why
every day at 5 I would get whipped till I was
red and made go to bed
since THE LORD walks with me every day
know every day at 5 I do not have to live
the same way

Struggle The Same

Sometimes in life everyone
must go through some kind of struggle in life,
now not everyone`s struggle will never be the same,
but just about all struggle will bring you pain!
When you struggle in life that makes you appreciate what
you have,
and also where you have been in your life,
and like I said no one's problems will never have the same
blame,
but the struggle can sometimes feel the same!
Whatever you do, don`t let the struggle get the best of you,
sometimes this struggle can make you want to throw it all
in,
but when you feel like this
that is when your real struggle will begin,
and that`s how you will find your true friends,
is where your struggle starts and ends!

Soul Guard

People today run to the bank,
and lock all their money away
we put insurance on a car,
but what about insurance on your heart?
What you need to do today,
is let the Lord lock your soul away.
If God puts a guard on your soul,
the Devil will lose all control.
The Lord wants to put a guard on your soul today,
so why do you just keep turning Him away?
If your soul is not guarded by Grace,
your soul may in up in a bad place.
The Devil wants you to believe
you will live forever, and you will never die.
If I was you I would turn my life over to God,
because the Devil has been known to tell a little white lie.

A Pastor

A Pastor is here to tell us what God has to say,
but we still want to turn him away.
A Pastor will try to tell us what is right,
and will try to tell us what God has for us in sight.
A Pastor will try to tell the people what the Lord wants
them to be,
but some people still will say that life isn`t for me.
A Pastor is trying to let the people know,
that the Lord is the One running the show.
If you don`t listen to the Pastor today,
when you die you will see you went the wrong way.
When your Pastor comes before you today,
remember this is what God wants him to say.
When your life feels like no hope can be found,
remember the Lord is still here, and can turn it all around.

People Can Do

people can push me around
but THE LORD want let me stay down
people can tear my flesh
but my soul will rest
people will try to put a hole in my heart
but they cannot tear my soul apart
people try to make me look a shame
but THE LORD knows their name
people try to be cool
so they try to make someone else
look like a fool
after I die
people cannot touch me in the sky
if your soul is wrong
the devil has a seat for you on his throne

10 Signs of the Devil

Always mad no matter what the case,
and never wants to see a happy face.
Never wants to go to church to pray,
and don`t believe in God anyway.
Loves when homes are broke,
so they can start up a joke.
Very greedy and will not help people out,
and does not care what comes out their mouth.
Thinks everything is run by a man,
and will never except God`s plan.
Wants to hurt people and do crime,
and does not care if they get a lot of time
Always tells people do not believe in God,
because GOD is not in sight,
but when you die God will show you the light.

Birds in The Sky

birds in the sky
all they have to do is fly
fly all day
and living life day to day
birds can be any color in the book
but most people do not take time to look
birds will fly high in the sky
but you will never hear a bird lie
you will hear a bird make a lot of sounds
but most birds like to stay off the ground

Feel My Pain

My pain pours out like the rain.
The rain might stop today,
but I cannot find nothing to take this pain away,
how much pain can I bear,
and I wonder does anybody care?
Somebody needs to help with my pain,
before I go completely insane.
How much pain can I bear at one time?
I don`t know, but I`m about to lose my mine.
Someone needs to help me today,
take some of my pain away.
Sometimes I try put my pain aside,
but my pain is too much to hide.
Look in my eyes and you will see,
sometimes my pain is too much for me.

Happy 50 year Birthday

Congratulations you have made it 50 years,
and I bet you have shed a million tears.
Through all the good, and all the bad,
you never let life keep you sad.
How many more years can you go?
I guess only the Lord can know.
You have seen people live and die,
and sometimes you might ask the Lord why?
Why am I still here in this place,
I guess the Lord Isn`t ready for me to see His face.
When life seems to be getting you down,
remember your maker is still around.
Fifty-one, Fifty-two, Fifty-three,
how much longer will the Lord bless me.
You are 50 years young today,
so have yourself a Happy Birthday,
and remember to thank God for this day.

My Lord

My Lord I need you today,
before I throw my life away.
My life has been so hard,
but talking to you made it a lot better.
My Lord you are Great,
so please don`t let me end up in the Devil`s lake.
One day My Lord I want to stand with you,
but first you have to forgive me for what I do!
I`m not saying I`m the best,
but when I die please let my soul rest.
Now My Lord has showed me a better way,
and just in time cause I was going to throw my life away.
My Lord you are one of a kind,
and I`m glad you gave me a piece of mine.
My Lord help me conclude every day,
with me getting the Devil a lot further away.
Lord please have mercy on me,
when I come Your way,
and please don`t let my soul be the Devil`s pray.

Bad Situation

You got yourself in a bad situation today,
so, maybe you need to turn to the Lord and pray.
You are in jail with no bail.
Do you feel like you are all alone?
Do you wish you could just go home?
How much more time can you do?
If you trust in the Lord, He will see you through.
You have people that love you at home,
so you have no reason to feel alone.
I know you feel like you have thrown your life away,
but the Lord will give you hope to live day to day.
You are in a bad situation no doubt,
but the Lord is still waiting to help you out.
Turn over your body and turn over your soul,
and let the Lord Take control.

The Love

we have been together a lot of years
and we have also shed a few tears
I know my love for you is true
because all I can think about is you
I know our love will last till the end
because I can see where our love has been
the love I have for you in my heart
no person on earth can tear it apart
even through all this pain
my love will still fall like the rain
every time life lets you down
remember my love is still around
there has been times I wanted to throw
our love away but the love I have for you
would always make me stay
look in my eyes and you will see
the love I have for you will always be

Who Am I

Who am I in this land,
nothing but a common man?
Who am I just a man,
trying to live by God's plan.
Who am I today?
Just a man trying to live day to day.
Who am I in man's sight?
Just an ordinary man trying to live right.
Who am I in the Lord's eye?
A man's soul that needs to be saved before I die.
Who am I from town to town?
Just a common man that needs his soul found.
Who am I,
without following the Lord's plan?
Just another soul waiting for the Devil's frying pan.

Happy Birthday to my Wife

The Lord has blessed you with another year,
so thank God you are still here.
Sometimes life can get you down,
but remember my love will always be around.
How many more years can you go?
I guess only God can really know.
How many times in life can you fall,
it does not matter because God,
will be there through it all.
This is the day the Lord set aside for you,
so do not let nobody today make you blue.
Sometimes life can make you feel a lot of pain,
but the Lord can stop your pain, like he stops the rain.
So on this very special day,
have a Wonderful Birthday.

A Year Anniversary of 911

2 years have passed since that dreadful day,
no one ever thought that day would end that way.
A lot of innocent people died,
and a lot of people stood at broken buildings and cried.
What kind of people would try to tear our country apart?
I guess they didn`t have God in their heart.
This anniversary suddenly got the world wanting to pray,
but what about every other day.
How many people died on that day,
really no one can exactly say?
This year 911 is just not any number on the phone,
911 this year means someone want be coming home?
Could that day have turned out another way,
or was that a wakeup call for people today?

911 Part 2

Bodies and blood all over the place,
so much blood you couldn`t see some people`s face.
This is an anniversary like no other we have ever had.
This anniversary is about people we lost,
and how it made us sad.
One good thing happen on this day,
at least it made people stop and pray.
To the world today,
have a happy anniversary.
When you get ready to pray,
say one for the people that didn`t make it through that day.

Prove my Love

What do I have to do,
to prove my love for you?
How many ways can I prove to you,
that my love for you is true?
How can I prove that my love for you is very strong,
and I would never want to do you wrong?
I hate it when we fuss and fight.
Tell me how to get our love right?
I would do anything to prove my love today.
Please just do not take your love away!
Sometime we do not think the same way,
but that is not any reason to throw all this love away.
If I buy you a dozen roses and a bottle of wine,
will you say your love is still mine?
What will it take to prove my love,
or will our love fly away like a white dove?
To prove my love to you,
there is nothing on earth I would not do.

Tears of Shame

my tears fall like the rain
can someone tell me how to stop this pain
I have tears of shame
but am I to blame
I have tears of shame in my eyes tonight
tell me what I have to do to make it right
tears of shame in my eyes
I cannot go on living with these lies
tears of shame in my heart
tell me how do I tear this pain apart
sometimes I can be hot as fire
or sweet as heaven
and tonight I might stay out past eleven

A Son's Love

a sons love will always be his passing
was something you did not want to see
a sons love will show through it all
and in time your pain will fall
your son is in a better place
but I know you would like to see his face
all your sons suffering is gone
but I know you feel all alone
a sons love cannot be erased
and have comfort he is with GOD in grace
your son will be watching over you when
you sleep so there is no need to weep
your son's death was not in vain
because GOD has took away all his pain

8-28-2009

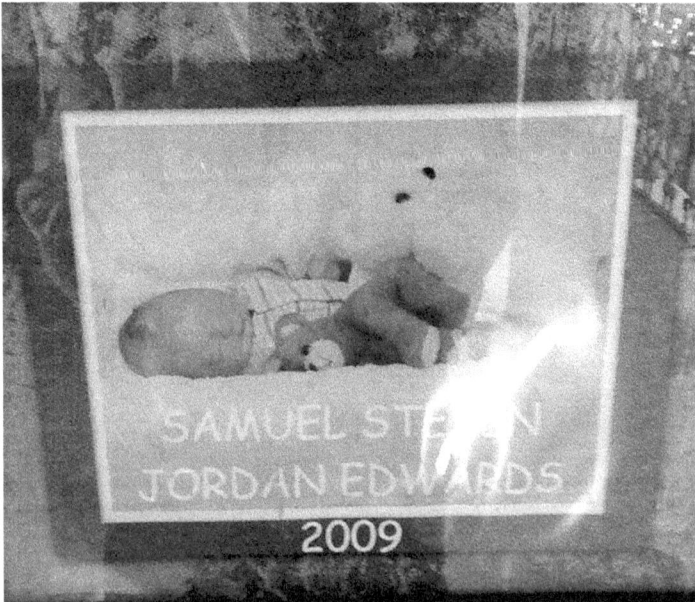

No Mom

No Mom no, is all I could scream,
when my Mother started to abandon me.
I said this must be a dream!
She will come back,
I know she will,
but it`s been a long time,
I wonder what is the deal?
Mom said she would pick us up the weekend,
but I don`t think Mom is coming,
how many years has it been?
No Mom I begged her not to go,
that was about 20 years ago!
No Mom I don`t understand,
how you could make that drastic of a call,
to throw your kids away,
liked you never loved us at all!
Mom if you read this I forgive you,
but that was a lot of pain you put us through!

You Got Some Explaining to Do

Baby tell me what I see isn`t true,
why do you make me go through the pain like I do?
Why do you make me go through this pain,
you better stop before I go insane!
I thought our love was true,
now look what you went and had to do.
I thought our love would always be,
but now that isn`t what I see.
Why did you go and tear our love apart,
now all I have is a broken heart.
It would be wise if you got out of my face,
cause I don`t know what I`m going to do,
without you in this place!
I`m tired of all the lies and deception,
tell me the truth I need a confession!
I`m about to put this gun in the air,
why did you have to take our love there?

Your Pride

your pride is something you cannot hide
your pride will not let you
put certain things aside that people do
even in gun play your pride
will not let you run away
your pride will not let you walk
when someone is talking that smart talk
even when you are telling lies
your pride makes it hard to idolize
your pride always wants to be right
even if you have to fight
some people will try to take your pride away
but keep holding your head up
and always remember to pray
if you try to mess with a person`s pride
you will see a person`s pride
is something that will not be denied

A Grandmother's Love

a grandmother's love will always be
I know her passing was something
you did not want to see
a grandmother's love will show through it all
and in time your pain will fall
a grandmother's love cannot be erased
and have comfort because
she is in a better place
no one can help with the pain you feel inside
because your pain must be too much to hide
your grandmother will be watching
over you when you sleep
and she would not want you to weep
no one can forget the smile
on your grandmother's face but now she
can smile in her eternal resting place
your grandmother is gone but do not be sad
just think of all the good
memories that you all had

Love and Lust

some people say they are one in the same,
but if you think that way you only have yourself to blame,
because lust will always look good at first,
but in the end that lust will be your biggest curse!
If you run into real love you will always know,
because when your eyes meet,
that is when your heart will skip a beat!
sometimes lust can make you feel as young as a child,
and make you lose your mine, and let yourself get wild,
just doing all kinds of crazy things to make this lust last,
because you are looking for a new love,
because the one you did love her love has gone on,
leaving the love between you and her in the past,
so that got me to thinking, is any love meant to last?
love and lust do you still think they are the same,
if you do, when your heart gets broke you only have
yourself to blame!

Steven W. Edwards

Happy Mother's Day

Mom Happy Mother`s Day
to you with all my love
the love I hold in my heart is above the rest
and sometimes our love has gone through the test!
I know we do not see each other like we want to,
but that don`t stop the fact that I love you!
No matter what you have done,
you will always be perfect to me,
and in my eyes that is how it will always be!
So Happy Mother`s Day, from your son,
with all the love in my soul!

When It's Over

When your life is over,
there is nothing left you can say!
I hope before you died you took time out to pray!
All you have done in this world you will answer for,
and all your pain and suffering on earth will be no more.
When it`s over that is the end of all of your fun,
now you will meet your Maker,
and you will have to answer for the wrong that you have done!
When it`s over I hope you don`t have to say,
God please don`t sent me to Hell,
I didn`t mean for my life to turn out this way!
When it`s over there is nothing left you can do!
I hope you had your life right and, God shows pity on you!
When the Lord is ready for you and calls your name,
will you be happy because you are going to Heaven,
and you have no shame,
or will you be ready to catch, that Hell bound train?

Hunt A Fish

Hunting or fishing, which one will it be?
When do you have time for me?
We have been together a lot of years,
and I bet you have killed a lot of deer.
In our life you have caught a lot of fish,
and I got you so I guess I got my wish.
How many hours are you going to fish today,
or can we go to the church and maybe pray?
You clean your gun,
and you're out the door ready to run.
You got your gun in your hand, your bullets and your bait,
and I'm behind you yelling at you to wait.
Hunting in the winter is all you want to do,
but when hunting season is over, I will still love you.
Even though you hunt and fish every day,
my love for you will never go away.

Nobody In Life

I`m tired of being a nobody in life,

having to go home to an unhappy wife.

I`m tired of being a nobody in life,

I'm down on the ground who people look down on.

I`m tired of being a nobody in life,

when people walk by,

they won't look me in the eye.

I`m tired of being a nobody in life,

that has no hope,

because I`m always broke.

I`m tired of being a nobody in life,

that only has a happy face,

when I have money to waste.

I put my problems in the Lord's hands,

and now God is showing me some different plans.

Now all I have to do any day,

is get on my knees and start to pray,

and God always takes my pain away.

Goodbye 2003

2003 has come and gone now 2004 will enter our home!
Good bye 2003 you was sure a crazy year,
but good bye because 2004 is here!
Good bye 2003 you are a memory forever more,
because the people are getting ready for 2004!
How many more good byes can we say,
not many because 2004 is coming our way!
2003 showed how crazy some people can be,
but get that crazy at the end of 2003!
Good bye 2003 we will never see you again,
now it`s time for 2004 to begin!
Good bye 2003 this is your last day,
because 2004 is pushing you out of the way!
Good bye 2003 you are like a burned
out light bulb that has to be replaced,
now 2004 will show its unknown face!
God be with us as we say good bye to 2003 tonight
and help us in 2004 to make everything all right!

Do You Believe

Do you believe in us,
or is our love not worth the fuss?
Do you believe this is a game,
or do our feelings feel the same?
Do you believe this is true love that was found,
or is our hearts just playing around?
Do you believe I would do anything for you,
or do you believe my love was never true?
Do you believe our love is worth a fight,
or will our love pass like the night?
Do you believe our love is worth all this pain,
or will our love eventually evaporate like the rain?

Run Daddy Run

How many daddies are out there today,
that will make a baby, then turn around and run away?
A Child didn`t ask to be born,
into this evil place,
but surprise look at this Child,
this Child has Your Face!
Not being there for Your Child,
will hurt Your Child in the long run,
because Your Child will never know their father,
and you will miss out on a lot of fun!
When you have a Child and run away,
is that being a man?
I think a Man wouldn`t take that cowardly way!
How many men love it when it`s time,
for them and a women to play?
So men we are support to hold up,
for our responsibility the same way!
Run Daddy Run,
abandon Your Child and have your fun,
but when you die you will have to answer,
for this wrong which you have done

Happy Birthday Jesus

Happy Birthday Jesus
You are the reason we are here today.
So we just want to say,
Happy Birthday Jesus.
When we stop and take time to pray,
we will not forget to say,
Happy Birthday Jesus.
Thank you for being born into this place,
and for dying for our sins and coming back,
and showing your face.
Happy Birthday Jesus,
because there was thing you had to die for,
now your people don`t have to live in sin anymore.
So one more time I would just like to say,
Happy Birthday Jesus,
and thank you for allowing us to pray.

I Know A Man

I know a man that can help you on your way,
but you must be willing to pray.
I know a man that will never run away,
no matter what problems is in His way.
I know a man that can erase all of your sins,
and peoples souls is what he mends.
I know a man that would like to see your face,
when it`s your time go to God`s heavenly place.
I know a man that can make it rain,
and that same man can also take away your worldly pain.
Who is this man I speak of?
His name is Jesus, and He was sent from up above.

Streets of Shame

There once was a lady,
that made her living,
by giving men pleasurable feeling.
Let me tell you this story, and maybe I can help you,
to see what being in them streets can do.
She has always made a lot of money,
but being in them streets is not funny.
She would sleep around from man to man,
just as long as they put money in her hand.
She is walking the streets in shame,
but is she really to blame?
There`s one thing this lady would always say,
five husbands can a man love me,
or is money the only love I will see?
She never knew where she would sleep from night to night,
but as long as a man will give her money,
she would always turn out alright.

XXXX Christ

when you do not want things in your way
you put a x on them
to let them know to go away
let's talk about Christmas day
why is that the only day
we want to pray
we put a x on Christ on his birthday
so why do we celebrate Christmas anyway
Christmas is support to be
about fun times and a lot of love and cheer
but always remember who died
so we could be here
the world may have a x
on Christ on this Christmas day
but if the world dies with that x
Christ will make them pay

Birthday Lady

I hope you are having a nice time on your birthday,
and I hope everything is going your way.
You are a special kind of Women,
because you do not mind lending a helping hand,
or helping out your fellow man!
When people are in trouble you are around,
but they better know you will clown.
You have a lot of love in your heart,
and that is something no one can tear apart.
The love we have for you is more than anyone could ever
say,
but our love for you grows stronger each and every day!
52 years is a lot to be thankful for,
and we hope you live to see 52 more!
So on this very special day,
have yourself a very wonderful Happy Birthday!

The Price

what is the price on your gift today
I want to know what they had to pay
if you do not hit your pocket book deep
your gift is too cheap to keep
how much are you going to buy me this year
is all at this time you will hear
a long time ago Jesus was born on this day
so did someone throw this day away
the only thing people do on Christmas day
is go to the store and want more and more
there is no price you can pay
no gift you can give
to repay Jesus for letting our souls live
Jesus died for you and me
and that kind of love is hard to see
so before you go to the store
on this Christmas day
stop and thank god for sending Jesus our way

A Sad Broken Heart

How can you fix a sad broken heart today
or do you say forget it and throw what you had all away?
How can you fix a heart that is sad?
I guess you will have to start,
by thinking about the good memories you had.
Do you know someone that can mend a sad broken heart,
or has our love grown too far apart?
There is one person that can mend a broken heart today,
but you will have to stop and take time out to pray!
A broken heart like this will be hard for you,
but there is nothing God can`t do!
If you have a sad broken heart,
and you feel like you want to throw your life away,
the only thing left is to try God and pray,
and I bet your sad broken heart will suddenly ease away.

Dr. Jesus

Who is this modern day medicine man,
that can heal your problems by touching His hand?
Dr. Jesus, Where is He?
This is the Dr. I need to see!
Where is His number I need to call,
because I do not feel well at all?
Dr. Jesus, Where have I heard that name?
Can He help me with my pain?
Dr. Jesus, I heard He made a blind man see!
Maybe this is the Dr. for me.
The Bible told of a woman, her bleeding wouldn't stop.
Dr. Jesus got a hold of her and she has not bled a drop.
There's one more thing the Bible said,
that Dr. Jesus can raise the dead.
Dr. Jesus was sent from above,
to show us God's love.
If you want to call Dr. Jesus today,
all you have to do is kneel down and pray.
Dr. Jesus will be on his way.

Unexpected Journey

If you take an unexpected journey
out of this world tonight,
would you be ready
and will you have gotten your soul right?
Unexpected journey you never know when that day will
come,
so get your heart right with God
and do not keep walking around
with a lost soul being like you are blind or dumb,
just waiting for your doom to come!
Unexpected journey who can say what day will be,
but if your heart is right with God
that will be a day you will long to see!
Do not take an unexpected journey to Hell
when you do not have to! God is here
He can save you,
but your heart with god must be true!

Fake or True

Are we fake or are we true?
When we give a person a smile,
knowing you haven't cared for them in a while.
Are we fake or are we true?
When we shake someone`s hand, and say how do you do.
Are we fake or are we true?
When we kneel down to pray,
or do us really what God in our life today.
Are we fake or are we true?
When we tell someone we have their slack,
and talk about them behind their back.
Are we fake or are we true?
When we go to church to be seen,
and not to get your soul redeemed.
Are we fake or are we true?
When we say I love you.

My Friend

My friend and I was good and tight,
we use to hang out about every night.
My friend called and said come hang out with me,
and I said not tonight but, maybe tomorrow we will see.
When the phone rung at 2:00a.m., I felt something bad,
but I wasn`t prepared to hear,
I had lost the best friend I had ever had.
Even though He is dead and gone,
in my heart His memory will still linger on.
My friend always liked to have a lot of fun,
but when trouble came He would not run.
My friend wouldn`t hold back on what He had to say,
and if He was here today, He would still be the same way.
I sometimes say My Lord, why wasn`t this me,
because losing a friend was hard to see.
When the nurse came in and said, there`s nothing we can do,
it`s like a part of me died with them words to.
Lord please show me something good ahead,
because I don`t know how I can make it with my friend dead.

Angel In Heaven

The Devil was once an Angel in Heaven.
He was even one of God's chosen seven.
The Devil saw the power He could possess,
so He wanted to take over and make Heaven His nest.
A third of God's Angels turned to the Devil's side,
but God didn't run away and hide!
God and the Devil had a big war,
and now the Devil does not live in heaven anymore.
God cast the Devil and His Angels into the lake of fire,
and said is this what you desire?
Everyone that turns their heart from Me,
Hell is where your soul will be.
Everyone that does not kneel down and pray,
the lake of fire is where your soul will stay.
Now the Devil will do what He can,
to get you to hell and to turn you away from God's plan.

A Good Day

What would be your idea of a good day,
one with no worries or problems in the way,
maybe your idea of a good day
is a day of shopping at the mall,
or just giving your mom or dad a call,
or maybe it will be just hanging out with a friend,
or maybe it is trying to make a brand new love begin,
but whatever is may be, make sure you have a lot of fun,
because most of the our lives are always under the gun,
so every now and then stop and have you a good day,
and your day will always be good if you take time and pray,
because God will already remove all the bad out of your way,
so now all you will have to do is smile and have a good day!
Now days a good day a million dollar dream,
you have it so close at hand,
and always someone or something is always there to ruin the
plan!

Heaven or Hell

Heaven or Hell, Which one do you want to see?
I think Hell is too bad for me!
Heaven or Hell, The choice is at hand,
but the only way to get to Heaven,
is by following God`s plan!
Heaven or Hell, Do you want to follow God,
to His promise land,
or follow the Devil,
to Hell like every other sinful man?
Heaven or Hell, It's not a hard decision to make,
but how much longer will God wait?
Turn to God and He will never fell,
or turn to the Devil,
and listen to the lies He has to tell.
Heaven or Hell,
I can`t answer that question for you,
but Heaven is where I want my soul to go to.
The only way you will see God`s promised land,
Is to give your life to God,
and be kind to your fellow man.

Eyes Of a Child

My life as a child was hard for me to bare,
sometimes it felt like,
my own Mother Didn`t even care.
I was moved around from place to place,
and I sometimes wonder,
was my life just one big waste?
How I survived was hard to say,
I`m glad the Lord Didn`t throw me away!
Looking through the eyes of a child,
can be very sad.
Now tell me where is the love this child never had?
You think about things that has past,
why must a child`s love be put last?
How many tears must a child cry?
Please don`t wait until it`s too late,
to say good bye!

Hard To Make It

It's hard to make it to Heaven,
and easy to make it to Hell!
If you want to make it to Heaven,
there are some things you must do.
First you must follow God,
and your heart must be true!
It's hard to make it to Heaven,
but Jesus has shown us a way,
but we must be willing to pray!
If Heaven is what you are seeking for,
turn your heart to God and, you will seek no more!
Hell is where nobody intends to go,
but if you turn your heart from God,
this is sure to be so!
It's hard to make to Heaven,
living in this sinful world today!
The only way to make it to Heaven is to,
turn your heart to God

Where Is God

Where is this God
you talk about all the time,
He must be just in your mind?
No, God is real I tell you,
but where are you looking?
Maybe you are looking in the wrong place,
because I tell you God is right in your face!
So where are you looking anyway,
did you try to pray,
or do you need someone to show you the way?
Where is God,
He is waiting to come into your heart
and take some of your pain away,
and all you need to do is pray,
and the Lord will always be on His way,
so where is God you ask me,
He is all around us,
so open up your heart, so you can see!

Come Back Famous

If I come back famous,
would that make you notice me?
Or will there be something else,
wrong with me you will see?
If I come back famous,
and go on a big time talk show,
I guess you will be the first to want to go.
If I come back famous,
then will you love me,
or is there something else,
wrong with me you will see?
How could you abandon your child,
at that young of age?
Give them over to strangers,
never thinking about the brain dangers!
If I come back famous,
I guess that is the only way I can get to you,
I guess that is a small price to pay to hear,
the words I love you!

God Made

God made everything on earth
to be free, as far as
our eyes can see!
God made the Heaven`s and the earth,
then made man and then a woman to give birth!
God made this earth for you to Rome around,
in hope our soul may be found!
God made you, so He knows sometimes you will fall,
but when you do just give Him a call!
God made Hell and that is where all the none believers go,
but for you, this does not have to be so,
because God made a way out of Hell too,
but first you must give your life to God,
and your heart to God must be true!

Don't Cry For Me

Don't cry for me,
because all my pain is gone,
and my soul can finally go back home.
Don't cry for me,
I will be alright,
you just try to get your soul right.
Don't cry for me,
because I'm going home,
to sit with God on His throne.
Don't cry for me,
and please don't look sad,
Just remember all the good memories we had.
Don't cry for me,
or sing any sad old song,
because now my soul can finally go home.
Mom, don't cry for me,
because I will see you again,
But for now, me and the Lord,
Are going to take it on in.

Mad At Me

If you get mad about what I write, then you need a talk with
God,
because He always knows what best for you,
when you really don`t have a clue,
when you get mad when someone tells you right from wrong,
that means there is still hope for you,
but you must stop what you do,
before anyone can even try to help you!
when you are living your life like there`s nothing going on,
pretending you do no wrong,
how can your soul get home?
but as long as you want to change a change will come,
but I hope it`s sooner than later for some!

Always Good

when you start a new love you will always
think it is always good,
but that is how all love starts out,
but you will think very different when
nothing but lies come out their mouth,
or you are paying their bills and they put you out,
that kind of love will make you shout!
Just when you think about giving in,
she will turn into your best friend,
and then the drama will start all over again,
then you will wonder what happen to my friend!

Give Thanks

This year let's stop and give thanks to God
for all in our life He has done,
and for allowing us to live life and have some fun!
This year just don`t be about what you can get,
because you will just be living your life in such regret!
This year give thanks to God, and please try to help someone out,
and don`t let so many bad words come out of your mouth!
This year give thanks to your maker for just keeping you around
and try to keep your feet on solid ground!
This year don`t always let everything be about you,
show someone you have love in your heart too!

Take Away my Pain

Lord take away this pain I feel every day,
because I cannot find nothing to make it go away,
Lord it`s like I`m living my life in vain,
trying to get rid of this pain,
will my pain ever go away,
maybe I need to pray,
My Lord I`m doing bad and always feeling sad,
because I miss the love of a lifetime I once had!
So Lord I`m here on my knees asking you to help me make a
change,
but I know a change must come from within,
but right now Lord you are my only true friend!
Look in my eyes and you will see,
without you my Lord my pain is too much for me!

The Life You Live

The life you live will always follow you
no matter what in life you are trying to do!
You can run from the past,
but your running will never last,
because sooner or later someone will find you,
then all your running will be through,
then you are back to where you started
with nothing more you can do!
The life you lived you can never leave it behind,
but if you start to follow God your life will seem just fine,
so now you know about life and the way you live it,
so each day should be a change even if it`s just a little bit!

Gift Of Love

Everyone in life has a gift of love,
because Jesus gave it to us from above,
so what would you say your gift of love would be,
mine is trying to get people to Heaven, so follow me!
The only way to find your gift of love,
is you must first look deep inside your heart,
then God will show you what to do,
even when you don`t have a clue,
but if you get lucky and find the gift of love,
then you will have the secret to a good life,
like a husband or a loving wife,
whatever your gift is you will have to find it on your own,
and then you will find the road that leads you home!

That's Life

It`s funny about life,
how you can just be talking to someone one second,
and then getting ready to bury them the next,
and most people will just say that`s life,
and that`s just how life goes,
and why it happens a certain way nobody knows,
it must be the way God has chosen!
but just because the end of one life has come,
that is no reason for you to live your life in vain,
by holding on to the past, because their life has come and
gone,
so don`t live your life still trying to hold on!
anytime you talk about a loved one that has passed away,
everyone will always say that`s life,
but there must be more to it than that,
because how can a life just fade away,
life they never even lived one day!

Inside a Man's Mind

If you could look inside an old man`s mind,
I wonder just what you would find?
I bet you could see things that you never seen before,
and I bet there is a lot of crazy things you could explore!
If you look inside an old man`s mind
just think what you might see,
how to solve problems
and how to live life and to what degree,
there is no telling what kind of knowledge you will find,
if you explore the inside of an old man`s mind!
You might have a question you never knew the answer to,
and going inside the mind will be the only way to show you!
If I look I wonder what kind of history I will be able to see,
and how the mind handles problems and to what degree!
If I could see inside an old man`s mind
that would be a lot of knowledge I could gain,
but would my brain ever be the same?
If I look inside at an old man`s mind,
I just wonder just how far would I be behind?

So Called Christian

So called Christian with your nose in the air,
come on now really do you think that's fair?
Judging people wrongly just because they are poor,
really do you think you will ever see Heavens door?

Life Today Tomorrow Yesterday

Life today and tomorrow and yesterday,
should not always be the same,
but if it is who can you really blame,
if you walk down the street,
you should be proud to see someone when they call your
name,
and you should not have to hold your head down in shame!
So life today or tomorrow and yesterday should never be the
same,
but if it is, you only have yourself to blame!

Lover's In Love

If you are a lover in love,
that love is all you can think of,
but sometimes that is not such a bad thing,
but sometimes love can play some crazy games,
but love sometimes don`t play so easy,
because each time you want to play,
there is always something in your way,
but if you're in love bad enough,
believe me you will always find away!
Some may be good and some might be bad,
and some will be that love wish you never had,
and then there is that love that
you don`t know if it was good or bad!

Always Maintain

Always maintain in life no matter what you decide to do,
because there is always someone waiting to pull a trick on
you,
but if you have been tricked before and you maintain,
you should know exactly what to do!
Sometimes in your life it can take some unexpected turns,
and it will leave you feeling lost and blue,
not knowing what in life you can do,
when you are feeling like this,
there is only one person that can help you in life
no matter what your heart feels or desires to do,
God will always be there to help you!
Now days people say they are too far gone,
so they might as well just carry on,
but I tell you, this is not true,
because whatever you are going through,
God can reach down and save you,
and if you don`t believe me then try God for yourself,
and you will see He will never let you down,
and He will even turn your frown upside down!

Hung on The Cross

Hung on the Cross,
It was a murder on display,
because what crime did Jesus commit anyway?
How many men beat Jesus,
before He was hung on the Cross?
How much blood do you think Jesus loss?
Even while the men beat Jesus black and blue,
He still ask God to forgive them,
because they didn`t understand what they was about to do.
Hung on the Cross,
with thorns in His head,
Jesus was still not ready to give up His life to become dead.
Jesus voluntarily gave up His life,
on that Old Rugged Cross,
so people`s soul don`t have to take that big loss.
Hung on the Cross,
with murders, crooks and, thieves, could this be real?
I think Jesus got the rough end of this deal!

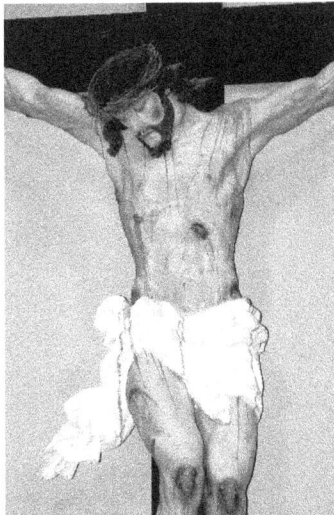

ABOUT THE AUTHOR

My Name is Steven Edwards. I was born in Jackson, MS in 1974. I grew up poor financially but rich in the love of my mother, grandparents, and other family including two sisters that are my world. There are a lot of things in my life that I'm not proud of. Getting saved was the greatest thing to ever happen to me. I know many people will be surprised of what I'm doing. All praise goes to God! I love going to church and I love serving God.

Writing has always come easy to me. It has exploded with God on my side. I now live in Okolona, MS. I am surrounded by plenty of friends and family that love me. Five years ago I lost my son. I thought everything was over, But God brought me through it. I hope this book will bring you through. If it doesn't wait for the next one. I have a whole series to bring you.

A SPECIAL THANKS

Now that you have read this book. I hope you see how God took a nothing and turn him into something. He did this just by the stroke of a pen. I was adopted and in and out of boys homes. I guess you can say I had a hard life. I never knew my father, I was taken away from my mother, beaten almost every day and always told I would be in prison by 18. I was talked about and always the last to be picked. I still made it because of God and you can to. God is fighting with you, and he loves you.

I would like to thank the "Poverty Clay Church". In 2009 they came to the hospital and paid for my son's funeral. He died at childbirth. They paid for his lovely casket and funeral. Donna, his mother and I thank you. It meant the world to us. Though we're not together we will always share our son's memory.

To Hannah. I still love you too. To the many people I did wrong and to God in Heaven I say I am sorry. God is not through with me yet. I love everyone that reads this book. I hope it will get you closer to God. Always pray for me. I will pray for you.

To my Son, Daddy will always love you. One day I will see you in heaven. That is my promise. Until then say, "Hello" to Jesus for me.

~Samuel Steven Jordan Edwards~

8-28-2009